Alexander Gilmore Cattell

**To Cuba and Back in Twenty-Two Days**

Alexander Gilmore Cattell

**To Cuba and Back in Twenty-Two Days**

ISBN/EAN: 9783337379292

Printed in Europe, USA, Canada, Australia, Japan

Cover: Foto ©Andreas Hilbeck / pixelio.de

More available books at **www.hansebooks.com**

# TO
# CUBA AND BACK

—IN—

## TWENTY-TWO DAYS.

A. G. C. Jr.

FROM THE PRESS OF THE

TIMES PRINTING HOUSE,

610 Chestnut St., Philada.

1874.

A Series of Five Articles originally
contributed to

"THE BEACON,"

A Monthly Amateur Journal of

Merchantville, N. J.

And, after some slight revision, published
in this form for

Private Circulation Only.

# *TOPICS.*

# TO CUBA AND BACK

## —IN—

## TWENTY-TWO DAYS.

### CHAPTER I.

Introductory.—Departure of the "Crescent City."—Our Companions.
—Seasickness.—Amusements.—The Sabbath.—A Memorable Dinner.—
First Glimpses of Cuba.—Morro Castle.—Havana.—The land-locked
Harbor.—View from Steamer's Deck.—Waving Palms.—The Fleet of
Boats.—Luscious Fruit.

THURSDAY, November 27th, we bid adieu to
Cuba, its tropical greenness and beauty; five
days later we see the snow-clad highlands of
New York and are chilled by winter's icy
breath. In visiting the "Queen of the Antilles," the land of orange grove and palm, a long-
cherished desire has been gratified, and our fullest
expectations met in its strange sights and luxuriant
growth; our enjoyment marred only by the sad, sad
picture of "Man's inhumanity to man," the cruelty,
ignorance and degradation so prevalent throughout
the Island of Cuba. Returning to the United States,
more than ever do we appreciate the blessing of civil
and religious liberty; and deeply grateful are we that
our lot has been cast in a Christian land. Desirous
of sharing with others our delightful recollections, and
hoping to impart pleasure and information, we attempt
a description of the scenes and incidents connected
with our trip TO CUBA AND BACK IN TWENTY-TWO
DAYS.

A journey of thirteen hundred miles· is before us; but unmindful of ocean's perils, with joyous anticipations, we make our preparations for the voyage. The steamer *Crescent City*, of Clydes' New York and Havana line, is our choice; and on Tuesday, November 11th, shortly before the time of departure, we are on board.

A hurried glance at the elegant spacious cabin and our cozy state-room, confirms all we have heard in praise of the *Crescent City*, which, just from the ship-yard of Messrs. Cramp & Sons, Philadelphia, is practically new, and this her first voyage to Havana. Ascending to the deck, we stand watching the busy and interesting scene presented.

All is activity aboard the steamer, while upon the crowded pier confusion seems to reign. Amongst the many attracted by the departure of the *Crescent City*, we notice Mr. Thos. Clyde and his son William P. Clyde. They move restlessly about, in consultation with captain, engineer or stevedore; here and there, on steamer or pier, infusing their energy into all with whom they come in contact. Such men should be and are a source of pride, assisting as they do in the rapid development of our country. Few of our readers are aware of the vast extent of their operations. In addition to this route (their latest venture), they have established lines from Philadelphia, New York and New Orleans to nearly every seaport on the Atlantic coast. Owning over fifty steamers, with a small army of employees, everything is conducted with system and dispatch. This personal attention to business—the great secret of their success.

From a vessel at our side we are receiving ponderous castings—machinery for the sugar-mill of some Cuban plantation—their transfer to the deck of our steamer proves quite tedious, being attended with considerable difficulty.

At last all is in readiness, our fastenings are cast off, and—amidst loud hurrahs—the *Crescent City* glides from the pier, much to our gratification and to the relief of the Messrs. Clyde, whose anxiety has been that nothing should occur to prevent the prompt departure of the *Crescent City*, their pet steamer.

With prow seaward we wend our way through the numerous shipping in the harbor. Onward we go; night is fast approaching; the lights of the great city grow less and less distinct, until all is shrouded in darkness; and, chilled by the cutting wind, we seek the warmth of our cabin; not, however, before Sandy Hook is passed and we are gently rocked by old ocean, causing us to realize that we are now fairly on our way to Havana. An hour later supper is announced; seated at the table we learn who are our *compagnons de voyage ;* nearly every face bears a foreign imprint, but some are unmistakably American. There is no sociability, as just now each seems to realize the dignity of his or her position, and nothing beyond the coldest civilities are exchanged. Supper ended, drowsiness comes over us; and retiring to our state-room, in blissful ignorance of the rising storm, we soon fall asleep, only to be awakened by the violent motion of the steamer as she plunges forward and is tossed by the angry waves. Morning appears, the storm rages even more fiercely, there is no inducement to arise, and we remain in our berth, nearly every passenger pursuing the same course. "Misery loves company," and it is some comfort that we are not alone in our sufferings. Oh! seasick mortal! what language can describe thy pangs, as with mind and body racked thou first fearest death and then

longeth for the grim messenger to end thy miserable
existence. Fain would we draw the curtain over
Wednesday's experience, referring to it only as a
blank; Thursday dawns bright and clear, and the
welcome sunshine comes streaming in at the port-hole.
Springing from our berth and quickly dressing, we
hasten on deck; the bracing sea air imparts new life,
our lost appetite returns, and we gain courage to take
our place at the breakfast-table; at lunch and dinner
new faces appear, until around the supper-table all
are gathered.

Our experience of yesterday has created a bond of
sympathy; formality vanishes, and there is now
manifested a kind and friendly feeling which deepens
as the evening advances, and continues through the
remaining days of our voyage.

"Opposite Charleston, about seven hundred miles
on our way," responds the mate, as at 10 o'clock
Friday morning, we inquire of him our position. The
sun is asserting his power; we have a foretaste of
tropical heat; and right welcome is the cool evening.

After supper we receive a Spanish lesson from our
instructor, a Cuban, and before retiring have made
some slight progress in the charming language.
Saturday the awning is spread, and beneath its grateful shelter gather the passengers, reading or convers-
ing, while many indulge in cards or chess, and a
game of quoits is in progress played with blocks of
wood—an indulgence of our kind and obliging Ship's
Carpenter. The ingenuity of all has been taxed to pro-
vide entertainment; each day has brought its variety
of enjoyment; and the time has flown so quickly that
that it seems but yesterday our voyage commenced.

Sunday our eyes open upon a day of surpassing

loveliness; through the port-hole we drink in the delightful morning air and catch a glimpse of Florida, the first land we have seen since leaving New York; visions of orange groves and magnolia come crowding before our mind, but all we now see is a barren waste, and none of its charms are revealed to us, not even when on deck as with the Captain's glass we scan the uninviting coast.

After breakfast we are afforded great amusement by a large school of porpoises, swimming just at our steamer's prow. Standing directly above them, we watch their every movement as they gaily disport themselves—maintaining their position with ease—until a pistol is discharged, and the ball striking the leader he immediately dives beneath the surface, the rest disappearing with him.

Deeply interesting also the flying-fish so constantly appearing and the myriads of Nautiluses or "Portuguese men-of-war" looking so beautiful in the sunlight.

Notwithstanding the charm and novelty of our surroundings, our thoughts turn, this Sabbath morning, to the loved ones at home. Gladly would we accompany them to the house of God. There will be no service aboard; but a few Americans retire to a state-room and there with united hearts we invoke God's presence and blessing, and afterwards rejoin our fellow-passengers, most of whom are utterly regardless of the sacredness of the day.

It is rumored that the dinner to follow, being the last on board, will excel all previous efforts; at lunch we partake lightly, and at four-and-a-half o'clock, with keen appetite are able to show our full appreciation of the magnificent dinner set before us; many are the thanks expressed for the generous provision which had enabled our able steward, Mr. Packard, to present so attractive a bill of fare.

---

*Sunday, November 16th, 1873.*

## NEW YORK AND HAVANA DIRECT MAIL LINE,

### STEAMSHIP CRESCENT CITY.
#### T. S. CURTIS, COMMANDER.

### BILL OF FARE.

#### ——SOUP.——
A la Reine.       Oyster.       Julliene.       Tomato.

#### ——FISH.——
Boiled Bass, Egg Sauce.       Boiled Halibut, Anchovy Sauce.
Boiled Codfish, Oyster Sauce.

#### ——ROAST.——
Saddle of Mutton and Currant Jelly.       Beef.       Chicken.
Pork.       Goose.       Spring Lamb, Mint Sauce.
Young Pig, Apple Sauce.       Baked Ham, Champagne Sauce.

#### ——BOILED.——
Veal.       Stuffed Turkey, Cranberry Sauce.
Chicken, Parsley Sauce.       Mutton, Caper Sauce,
Pig's Jowls and Cabbage Sprouts.
Corned Beef and Cabbage.       Corned Pork and Turnips.

#### ——GAME.——
Canvas-Back Duck.       Wild Pigeon.       Teal Duck.
Mole and Mallard Duck.       Saddle of Venison.
Prairie Chicken.

#### ——ENTREES.——
Chicken Salad.   Potato Salad.   Lobster Salad.   Fried Oysters.
Chicken Saute and fine herbs.       Boiled Squab on Toast.
Lamb Cutlets, Aux Petite Pois.       Prairie Chicken.
Potted Pigeon.   Lobster Plain.   Calves' Head, Brain Sauce.
Fricassee Chicken.       Calves' Feet, en tortu.

#### ——VEGETABLES.——
Mashed Potatoes.       Celery.       Tomatoes.
String Beans.   Onions.   Green Corn.   Parsnips.
Lima Beans.   Carrots.   Lettuce.
Green Peas.       Asparagus.       Baked Sweet Potatoes.
Turnips.       Squash.

#### ——DESSERT.——
English Plum Pudding, Stewed Sauce.
Squash, Apple and Cranberry Pie.
Madeira Wine Jelly.       Tipsy Parson.
Boston Cream Cake.       Lemon Ice Cream.
Blanc Mange.       Charlotte de Russe.       Jelly Tarts.
Candied Fruits.   Peaches.   Prunes.
Figs.       Nuts.       Raisins.       Grapes.       Apples.

#### COFFEE.
#### CHAMPAGNE AND TABLE WINES FREE.

Our repast ended, we gain the deck just as the sun is setting. The golden orb as it sinks behind the western horizon, gilds the heavens with its departing glory, the whole scene reflected by the placid waters; darkness quickly follows, revealing the phosphorescent light shining this evening with unusual brilliancy; we seem ploughing our way through a sea of fire, and every wave is tipped with silvery light, while the heavens are resplendent with lustre, beaming from starry worlds. Yielding to the fascination of this lovely and peaceful tropical evening, the passengers linger long on deck. Our pleasant intercourse is soon to end, and saddened by thoughts of the separation which will come with the morrow, we are reluctant to say "good night." Onward presses our noble steamer, fast nearing the coast of Cuba. We could drop anchor in the Bay of Havana before dawn, did not Spanish law forbid the entrance of any craft between sunset and sunrise; a law so inviolable that were we fleeing from the fury of a hurricane, still would deny us the safe shelter of the harbor. We are anxious to be up bright and early, and retire with the assurance that we shall not be forgotten. Awakened by the promised knock at our state-room door, our toilet is quickly made and we reach the deck before the sun has risen. We are now abreast the island, and its long line of distant hills is dimly outlined in the gray morning light; soon we observe signs of life in the fishers' villages by the water's edge, and can see them launching their tiny boats. Just before us, against the bright blue sky, looms up the tower of Morro Castle.

Next we distinguish the outlying portion of Havana

—to the extreme right La Punta Fort, while more prominent is the massive white-walled prison just beyond. A cannon upon the fortress breaks the stillness of the morning with its loud report, proclaiming that we are privileged to enter the harbor. Soon rounding the Morro Castle, almost grazing its rocky base, our prow is turned toward the narrow channel, and saluting the fort as she glides by, the *Crescent City* rides upon the quiet waters of the land-locked bay. At this moment a beauteous scene is presented; before us is Havana, its strangely-colored buildings, and tiled roofs, while in the background are low hills covered with tropical vegetation of richest green; the tall, graceful palm, standing out boldly, overtowering all. To our left stretches the long line of Cabañas fortifications, and in the distance the village of Regla. Turning again to the right we look upon Havana and its crowded shipping flying the flag of nearly every nation; but we must drop anchor and await the coming of Custom House and Health Officers, before steaming further up the bay. We see pushing out from the shore, and hastening toward us, numerous boats which soon surround us, and we are almost deafened by a loud chorus of boatmen's voices begging in Spanish or terrible English, the privilege of carrying us and our baggage ashore. Now arrive small sail-boats having aboard hotel runners who beseech and almost demand our custom for "San Carlos," "Santa Isabel," "La Inglaterra," or "Hotel El Telegrafo."

We hear the shrill cry "Naranja," "Naranja" (oranges, oranges), and displaying some silver coins, quickly receive in exchange a bounteous supply.

And now, beneath the awning, sheltered from the
sun's scorching rays, we enjoy the luscious sun-
ripened orange, while our eyes feast upon the strange-
ly-beautiful scene before us: waving palms, placid
water, quaint Havana; a scene more lovely than
ever our imagination had pictured; a reality far
exceeding our brightest dream.

## CHAPTER II.

UR delightful voyage from New York ended, the *Crescent City* drops anchor in Havana harbor, and soon we shall enter yonder quaint looking city. We are awaiting the arrival of the health officer, whose visit is necessary before we can leave the steamer. Intensely interested in our strange and beauteous surroundings, we do not share in the impatience manifested by our fellow-passengers at his delay. Now our attention is directed to a six-oared boat, flying the Spanish flag, rapidly approaching, beneath its awning sit the Custom House and health officials ; reaching the deck of our steamer, they are met by the Purser, who reports all well, and presents the ship's papers, which receive a hasty glance, our permit to land is signed, and the ceremony is concluded. All restrictions being removed, we are jostled and crowded by numerous visitors from the little boats about us ; runners from the hotels pressing us sorely for our custom. The welcome sound of the gong is heard and we descend to the saloon for breakfast. Seated opposite to us at the table, is Mr. McKellar, Clydes' Havana agent, who has come aboard this morning to pay his respects to Capt. Curtis, and to inspect our splendid steamer, which he pronounces a great accession to the line. Advised by him we decide to patronize the "Hotel el Telegrafo," and after breakfast are introduced to the representative of that hotel, who promises to accompany us there. A last glance at our cozy state-room, a hurried adieu to kind friends, and we follow our guide into the boat which is to carry us ashore; our baggage follows. Now all is ready, the boatmen bend to their oars, a breeze fills the sail and away we go, fairly bounding over the water, toward the custom-house, a half-mile distant, where all foreigners must land.

Arrived there we are assisted by our guide, who acts as interpreter; without unnecessary delay our baggage is examined, and we receive our passport, properly *vised*. Passing through the gate we step into a cab and are rapidly driven through the narrow, alley-like streets towards our hotel, a succession of novel sights meeting our view as we dash along. The low buildings, painted blue, pink or yellow; the barred windows of the dwellings; the shallow stores, entirely open in front; the odd vehicles; the people; their dress; everything so strange,

We find the "Hotel el Telegrafo" three-storied, with a projecting front, supported by stone pillars, and underneath a long line of show cases, filled with jewelry; passing inside we register, and are shown to our room, a spacious apartment with high ceiling and tiled floor, which proves to be splendidly situated, the low window opening out upon a balcony, from which we have a fine view of Havana; while just across the street, in the public parade-ground, known as "El Campo de Marte," a market-place greets our vision.

At once becoming interested in the scene before us, we are not content until, descending to the street, we cross over and mingle with the motley crowd of negroes, Chinese and whites moving about, the murmur of whose voices is comparable only to the confusion of tongues at the Tower of Babel.

In the booths, exposed for sale, are large piles of golden oranges, immense quantities of bananas, and heaps of yams, dates, guavas, pineapples and cocoa-nuts; also, a great variety of fruits and vegetables entirely new to us.

Fain would we linger, but the odor arising from decayed matter upon which shines the rays of a noon-day, tropical sun, hastens our departure, and we return to our room, satisfied that " distance lends enchantment to the view."

Now taking a cab we visit the office of Mr. Mc-Kellar, 76 Calle-de-Cuba, the head-quarters of Americans in Havana, where we exchange our gold for Spanish currency, afterwards calling at the United States Consulate; thence to hotel, which is reached about 4 o'clock.

Prejudiced against Spanish cooking by what has been told us of their liberal use of oil, we have an agreeable surprise in the very enjoyable dinner provided. It is served in six courses; the dishes, while they are mostly strange to us, are very palatable; excepting, perhaps, the fried banana which needs an acquired taste. A dessert of delicate pastry, guava jelly and delicious fruit, followed by coffee, concludes the dinner; but we linger to watch the people seated at the little tables scattered about the dining-room.

Wine is seen in nearly every glass, and very many are smoking, either cigar or cigarette.

During the evening we see the city by gas-light, using again the four-wheeled, one-horse cab, of which there are over three thousand in Havana; charges regulated by law, being twenty-five cents to any point within the city limits, or one dollar per hour, if engaged " *tiempo* " (time).

We have greatly enjoyed our first glimpses of Cuban life afforded us in the visit to the market-place, and in our rides through Havana.

Before retiring, we step upon the balcony and look out over the city, now brilliantly illuminated—a fairy scene.

We retire, but not to undisturbed repose, as our couch is only a stout canvas stretched tightly over an iron bedstead, which proves decidedly uncomfortable.

"When in Rome do as the Romans,"—so we have resolved to follow the Cuban life, during our stay on the island. The daily programme of " Hotel El Telegrafo " is as follows :—

> *LUNCHEON at Early Morning, in Bedroom.*
>
> *BREAKFAST from 9 to 12.*
>
> *DINNER from 4 to 8 P. M.*

Accordingly, on awakening, we summon a servant and order naranja, platanos, el pan, la mantequilla, el café, (oranges, bananas, bread, butter, coffee,) which are quickly brought us and partaken of while dressing.

For to-day (Tuesday), we have planned a drive in the country to the village of Marianao about 12 miles distant; breakfast over, at 10 o'clock we start.

We are soon beyond the narrow streets of Havana, and upon the broad shaded avenue which leads to "El Cerro," a suburban village three miles out. To this point both sides of the avenue are lined with stores or dwellings, some of the latter very elegant, and with beautiful gardens attached; beyond "El Cerro," along the road are scattered small settlements, and Marianao proves to be a very insignificant village. We stop at its only hotel the "Nueva York," and having ordered a lunch, are ushered into a large room with tiled floor, in the centre of it a rug, around which are arranged, after the manner of the country, chairs facing each other; the waiter soon appears, and after spreading a clean white cloth, brings cheese, tongue, biscuit, butter and olives, also a generous plateful of fruit; then bringing some stalks of sugar-cane, he cuts them in pieces about six inches long, next pierces the eye of a green cocoanut, allowing the milk to drain into a pitcher. The lunch is ready— we have been greatly interested in its preparation, our eyes having fairly stood out as we watched the waiter's quick movements; the ride has given us a sharp appetite, and we enjoy everything set before us; extracting the juice of the sugar-cane we find it sweet and refreshing; of the cocoamilk, however, we do not partake freely, having been warned of a tendency to disagree with those unaccustomed to its use.

The country through which we have driven is truly

magnificent, all nature teeming with loveliness about us, the tall palm, cocoa trees, and a luxuriant growth of cactus, aloes and other tropical plants, with acres of bananas. We meet horses and mules, bearing upon their backs all sorts of burdens, baskets filled with fruit or vegetables, cages of live fowl, cans of milk, or bundles of sugar-cane; and we are greatly amused at the sight of a drove of horses in single file walking slowly beneath immense piles of corn-stalks, only their hoofs and the tips of their noses being visible.

We see lounging about, hordes of dirty negroes and white people, the very pictures of laziness; in fact, everybody seems half-asleep; and we are reminded of a holiday in the United States, when only a few are working, and those indifferently. Nature is indeed lavish in her gifts, but it seems only to promote a general disinclination for work. "Every prospect pleases and only man is vile."

We return to Havana by the same road, reaching our hotel after an absence of five hours, every moment of which has been enjoyed.

## CHAPTER III.

The Market-place.—"Los Molinos," the Captain-General's Garden.
—Laughable Scenes at a Fire.—Description of "La Honradez"
Cigarette Factory.—Visitor's Register.—The Cemetery.—The Bull-
Ring.—Women in Havana.—Theatre Tacon.—"El Louvre."—Lot-
tery.—La Dominica Fruit Preserving Establishment.—The Coming
Sabbath.

SO interesting the sights of Havana, so pleasant
our quarters at "Hotel el Telegrafo" that we
have been induced to prolong our stay until
Monday, when we shall leave for Matanzas,
stopping at Union, to visit a sugar-plantation
in the vicinity. We have found Havana decidedly
*foreign;* its architecture, streets, vehicles, people,
dress, language, customs, all so quaint and strange,
that we seem to be in some remote corner of the earth,
and can scarcely realize that our United States, the
land of progress and enterprise, is so near. The
temporary market on "El Campo de Marte" (field
of Mars), which our room overlooks, with its extensive display of Cuban products, and the motley
crowd in attendance, has been a source of unceasing
interest. By special permission of the Government
booths were erected by former occupants of the
principal market, recently destroyed by fire, involv-
ing a loss of several million dollars; to this mis-
fortune do we owe the pleasure derived from the
fascinating scene continually before us. During the
week we have thoroughly explored Havana, and
in addition to our drive to Marianao (already

described) have had frequent glimpses of the sur-
rounding country.

Just outside the city is " Los Molinos," the country
residence of the Captain-General ; to the magnificent
garden attached, visitors are admitted; and there we
spent a morning very pleasantly amidst the pro-
fusion of most exquisite tropical trees, plants and
flowers. Strolling about these grounds we discovered
a beautiful grotto and an artificial cascade emptying
into a lake, its shores lined with rank growth of
bamboo, but most charming to us, of all this lovely
picture, were the broad avenues of noble palms, whose
towering height denoted great age. After leaving
the Captain-General's garden, we visited " El Jardin
de Aclimatacion," and purchased a small collection
of plants, which we were assured by the proprietor
(a Frenchman) could be safely carried to our home in
Merchantville. Havana has a surprising number of
churches, the almost incessant clamor of whose
bells, commencing at early dawn, while it may serve
to remind the 210,000 inhabitants of their religious
duties, certainly becomes very monotonous to strangers. We have not been impressed with the grandeur
of the church edifices, the one designated "Cathedral
de la Virgen Maria de la Concepcion," a large an-
cient-looking structure, being attractive only as containing the remains of Christopher Columbus, the
great explorer, who on the 28th day of October, 1492,
discovered the Island of Cuba and shortly afterwards
the Western Continent. From history we learn that
Columbus died in Valladolid, Spain, May 20th, 1505,
the body was taken to Seville, 1513, thence in 1536
to St. Domingo, and on the 15th day of January, 1796,

was brought to Havana, and with great pomp and ceremony deposited in its present resting-place. At the left hand of the grand altar we were shown the tablet upon which is carved in alto-relievo, the bust of Columbus, and an inscription, which translated, reads:

> "O remains and image of the great Colon!
> Endure for a thousand ages, guarded in this urn
> And in the remembrance of our nation."

Ascending one of the towers we enjoyed a fine view of Havana, with its background of green-clad hills,— the far-famed land-locked harbor, its narrow entrance so well guarded by Morro Castle and La Punta Fort, and just beyond, stretching far away, the restless sea.

The numerous "Plazas," or public parks, with their noble specimens of palm and "Laureles de India" are striking features of Havana, vast sums have been expended in their adornment, many of them containing marble fountains, statuary, etc. During the evening music is discoursed at the "Plaza de Armas" and several other parks by the military bands, these "Retreta," or out-door concerts, being largely attended, even by the most aristocratic classes; the ladies appear in full dress, and usually remain seated in their carriages while listening to the music, though occasionally they may be seen promenading in company with their gentlemen escorts.

Happening one morning at a fire in the neighborhood of "Plaza de Armas," we had an exhibition of the excitability of these people; the frantic actions and misdirected efforts of the firemen were highly amusing, while the loud outcries which arose from the assembled multitude served to make "confusion worse confounded." Water was poured from buckets into the antiquated fire-engines, which were worked by hand, and long lines of men stood holding the hose above their heads, (the reason we fail to comprehend) these lines reaching to the scene of the fire, a two-storied stone building, to which the flames were easily confined, notwithstanding that, owing to the entire absence of discipline and concert of action, the greater portion of the water was thrown upon the people and otherwise wasted. Never have we laughed more heartily than while watching the excitement which this trifling fire had occasioned.

In Cuba smoking is universal, and to meet a person, young or old, who is not indulging in this national habit, is indeed a rarity. Tobacco is extensively cultivated on the island, and has a world-wide reputation for superior quality, Havana is the distributing point to other countries; and here is centered the manufacture of cigars and cigarettes. Havana has about one hundred and twenty-five manufactories of cigars, besides a number where cigarettes are made, everywhere "Fabrica-de-Tabacos" meeting the eye. "La Honradez," which occupies an entire block, is the largest cigarette factory in the world; regular days are appointed for resident visitors, but to "Americans" the doors are always open. We were treated with the utmost politeness and the workings of this vast establishment fully explained to us. On entering, by request, we registered our name, residence and occupation, after which we were placed in

charge of a very gentlemanly usher, who led us first
to the shops, where are made by machinery the boxes
and barrels; adjoining are a variety of machines,
the motive power furnished by an engine made in
Williamsburg, New York; next we visit rooms where
the tobacco is received and assorted, still further on,
where it is ground and afterwards, by hydraulic
pressure, formed into blocks of uniform size and
weight.

We examined some machines, of French invention,
capable of making fifty cigarettes per minute, but
almost too complicated to be of practical use. The
department of printing and lithographing proved of
great interest; here are produced for this factory vast
quantities of labels, wrappers, circulars, etc., many
of very tasteful design, and colored in the highest
style of the art.

In one room we saw about fifty Chinamen seated
at tables, engaged in packing the cigarettes in bundles of twenty-three or twenty-six each, according to
order. The quickness and precision with which the
requisite number are picked up and enclosed in the
wrapper was marvelous to us.

Besides the large force at work in the building,
(mostly Chinamen) the proprietors of "La Honradez"
employ the leisure moments of over two thousand
porters, servants and soldiers, to whom they furnish
the paper and tobacco, which is returned in "Tareas"
or rolls containing five thousand and sixty-four
cigarettes each. In the packing room is presented
a busy scene; while the production of "La Honradez" is over two and a half-million cigarettes
daily, so popular is this brand that there is never an

accumulation of stock ; boxes and barrels around us awaiting shipment were directed to almost every country in the world.

Returning to the office we were presented with a bundle of cigarettes and a printed copy of the "Visitor's Book," our name having been printed thereon while we were inspecting the factory. In this immense register we wrote opposite our name some comments on "La Honradez," which will be added to future editions of the "Visitor's Book," now numbering two hundred and ninety-seven pages, and containing thirteen thousand four hundred and sixty-seven names and comments, a few of which we present in illustration:—No. 6037, E. Lewis Quick, Broker, New York. (Recently of Merchantville.) "An immense concern and conducted with great ability." No. 13,167, J. S. Skinner, Broker, New Orleans. "This is indeed the most complete manufactory in every branch that I have ever seen, and a visit to Havana would not be complete without seeing it; my thanks are due to the firm." No. 12,991, J. W. Hopper, Engineer, New York. "I consider, after close observation, that this is the most complete tobacco manufactory in the world." No. 12,883, Henry Baldwin, Jr., Philadelphia. "The business, so organized that every detail of a complicated manufacture may be courteously and unreservedly submitted to the inspection and criticism of strangers, may well claim for its motto 'La Honradez,' ('honesty')."

No. 2496, William H. Seward, Secretary of State, Washington. "Deeply impressed with the successful manner in which the proprietor has combined *West*

*Indian* production with *American* invention, *European* talent and *Asiatic* industry."

Expressing our appreciation of the kindness shown us we depart, not, however, before we have purchased, in the retail department, some packages of cigarettes and smoking tobacco which we intend as presents to friends who are addicted to the use of the weed.

We have seen nothing more striking than the burial-place "Cementerio de Cristobal Colon," on the outskirts of Havana. It is divided by high stone walls into nine courts or hollow squares. The receptacles for the dead are niches, eighteen inches square, extending seven feet into the walls, in four rows, one above the other. Each court containing say nine hundred of these openings. After the corpse has been deposited (very often without a coffin), the entrance is closed by a slab, upon which is carved an inscription; in many cases a glass is placed in front, and in the space between (about three inches) is enclosed a wreath, crucifix or rosary. Not long since a party of young Cubans, students of the Havana Medical College, visited this cemetery; one of the number made a few scratches with his diamond pin on the glass at the tomb of Castanon, a Spanish general, which being discovered, seven promising young men were, by order of the Spanish government, cruelly shot. Doubtless our readers have full knowledge of the particulars, and that this dastardly outrage, a foul blot upon the civilization of the nineteenth century, met with universal condemnation.

A certain philosopher has said, "judge a nation by its sports." Spanish cruelty is proverbial, and the sports indulged in by the masses serve to cultivate

this characteristic. Cock-fighting is continually in
progress, while Sunday is reserved for the Bull-fight,
both being under Government patronage, highest
officials of the island lending their presence at these
most disgusting spectacles. We have had no incli-
nation to patronize the Cock-pit, nor shall we dese-
racte the Sabbath by attendance at the "Plaza de
Toros" or Bull-ring. We had, however, sufficient
curiosity to visit the building, a large wooden structure, seats arranged in amphitheatre form, with ring
in the centre entirely open to the sky. There are
private boxes, that of the Captain-General being
decorated with the Spanish colors. We were shown
horses which are ridden by the "Picadores" (Lancers); they have the appearance of worn-out stage
horses, poor, pitiable-looking beasts, far different from
the noble steeds our imagination had pictured. The
pantomime of our guide, with the descriptions pre-
viously given us by eye-witnesses, have enabled us
to clearly comprehend the manner of conducting
a bull-fight. The bull on entering the ring, is at
first confused by the shouts of the multitude, but
soon is aroused by the "Banderilleros" (dartmen
on foot), who display their red cloaks. The mounted
Lancers approach; now to further excite the bull,
sharp darts are thown by the "Banderilleros," and
not unfrequently "Fuego" are used, torpedoes which,
as they enter, explode and lacerate the flesh; and
now if the infuriated bull disembowels one of the
poor, blindfolded horses, the audience give every
manifestation of delight, in which join fair ladies and
children, and if the rider is gored, the entertainment
is considered even more rare; after the bull has been

sufficiently tormented, the "Matador" (swordsman) is summoned, who usually with one thrust slays the bull; the carcass is then dragged from the ring and a live animal substituted. Can we wonder that the estimate placed upon life is so slight, that cruelty is so prevalent throughout Spain and her possessions, when such scenes form a portion of the education of her people.

After our arrival in Havana, we first learned the fate of the captain and crew of the steamer "*Virginius.*" We have been painfully aware of the dislike and bitterness entertained against Americans by the Spaniards here, and the expression of our indignation would probably endanger life. Thursday the "*Virginius*" was towed into the harbor by the "*Tornado,*" its captor, their appearance has caused great rejoicing, and the principal streets are decorated with bunting, displayed in honor of the event. The "*Tornado's*" captain is the lion of the day, and a banquet has been tendered him by the "Casino," an organization of wealthy Spaniards, mostly slave-holders, which wields an immense political power on the island. Their club house, which we were privileged to visit, is one of the finest buildings in Havana, having cost several millions of dollars. The billiard room contains twenty-four tables, and there is a private theatre, with all the appointments, where performances are given for the amusement of the club and their guests.

The "*Tornado,*" a neat looking craft, is anchored just opposite the city, while the "*Virginius*" has been towed to the government arsenal, further up the bay.

We engaged a boatman, who rowed us alongside,

and thus had an excellent opportunity to inspect this noted steamer; she has two smoke stacks, and her model, long and narrow, with sharp prow, would indicate great speed; we cannot understand how she was overtaken by the "*Tornado*," seemingly to us, a much slower steamer. The grim sentries, pacing her deck, looked rather suspiciously upon us, and deeming "discretion the better part of valor," we did not linger long.

One rarely meets a female walking in the streets of Havana, excepting negresses, their turbaned heads and long trailed dresses affording us considerable amusement. Ladies here do not even leave their carriages when shopping, but the goods are brought out for their selection by salesmen. Our admiration is not excited by the faces of the Spanish or Cuban beauty; despite dark eyes, rich complexion, and regular features, their faces are uniformly expressionless; and we look in vain for indications of intelligence or strength of character which the faces of our ladies exhibit. When, in our morning drives, we pass the dwellings, we have observed, through the low, iron-barred windows, the careless and slovenly appearance of the inmates; and at evening, in driving past, noticed these same untidy creatures entirely transformed by their elaborate toilets. From our limited observation we should judge that the social position and privileges of the females are far below those enjoyed by the women of the United States. Very generally their education is neglected, and there are many in the highest walks of society whose knowledge of history, science, and literature is more limited than that of some American school-girls of thirteen.

The "Theatre Tacon," one of the finest opera
houses in the world, can seat about three thousand
people; the prevailing color of the decorations is blue,
and with cane-seated chairs, it presents a very cool
and inviting appearance, entirely in accord with this
"City of the Tropics." Just adjoining the "Theatre
Tacon" is "El Louvre," the fashionable café, where
one phase of Cuban life can be studied; vast crowds
congregate every evening, and a prodigous amount
of smoking and drinking indulged in. Some of the
drinks are peculiar to Cuba; we had been told to call
for "Panales Frio," and were brought a tumbler of
water and ice, across the top a delicate comb of sugar
and white of eggs, this we dissolved in the water, and
when a little lime juice was added we found it a very
pleasant beverage; but all are not of this harmless
character, brandy and other liquors being constantly
in demand. While admitting that but few cases of
drunkenness are met with in Havana, we must express
our conviction that the habitual use of wine by the
people of the island does not tend to their elevation;
its cost makes serious inroads upon the scanty earn-
ings of the laboring classes, depriving them of many
comforts they otherwise would enjoy; besides, as no
one will deny there are many instances where a
thirst for strong drink is acquired and the inevitable
ruin and sorrow follows.

The selling of lottery tickets affords a livelihood to
very many in Havana; everywhere we go these slips
of paper are thrust into our face, and we are constantly importuned by children, old men, or crippled
soldiers, to purchase a chance in the next drawing;
the hope of obtaining a fortune induces many to

invest their last dollar, in fact all classes are addicted to this species of gambling. Desirous of rewarding the head waiter at our hotel for his polite attentions, we handed him three dollars which we afterwards learned were almost immediately invested in a lottery ticket. Lottery is conducted by the government, notwithstanding the acknowledgment that it exerts a most demoralizing influence, not confined alone to Cuba but extending to the United States, where "Havana Lottery" is extensively advertised and its agencies established in the principal cities.

Should any of our readers visit Havana they must not omit seeing "La Dominica," an extensive manufactory of jellies, preserves and confectionery. We were shown the process of making their delicious Guava Jelly, so highly esteemed throughout the entire world. The Guava (a fruit resembling the orange, though smaller) is thrown into a caldron, and sugar added; after it has undergone the necessary cooking, being stirred meanwhile, it is strained, and poured while hot into wooden boxes of various sizes by Chinamen. A jam is also made from the Guava, which is much cheaper and very generally used as a substitute for butter, for be it understood that butter is a luxury unknown to a large majority of the inhabitants of Cuba, while the really good article cannot be found even at hotel tables, not excepting "El Telegrafo," the choicest New York butter yielding almost immediately to this climate. From the almost bewildering variety of preserved fruits offered by "La Dominica," we have selected a few jars, also some Guava jelly, quite certain that they will be fully appreciated by friends at home.

To-morrow (Sunday) we purpose attending early mass at the Cathedral, and will have the opportunity of seeing how the Sabbath is observed in Havana.

While we have endeavored to improve every moment of this week there are doubtless some places of interest which have escaped our notice, but our stay cannot be extended beyond Monday morning, when, as before mentioned, we leave for Matanzas, stopping en route at Union; our kind friend, Mr. McKellar, has favored us with a letter of introduction to a prominent machinist there, who will direct us to one of the numerous sugar estates in that neighborhood.   We shall proceed to Matanzas the same day; returning to Havana in time for the steamer " *City of Wilmington,*" for New York, sailing Thursday P. M. in which our passage has already been engaged.

## CHAPTER IV.

Sunday in Havana.—The Cathedral Services.—La Merced Church. —Leaving for Matanzas.—An Early Start.—Railroad Regulations.— Stopping at Union.—The Volante.—Our Visit to Sugar-Plantation.— The Machinery.—Slaves.—Coolies.—The Nursery.—Some Facts and Reflections.

ALTHOUGH not expecting that in Havana there would be the strictest observance of the Sabbath, we were somewhat surprised to find the day so generally disregarded; apparently there was no suspension of business amongst the cafés and retail stores, and a greater portion of the wholesale establishments were not closed.

In the afternoon crowds flocked to the "Bull-fight," and at evening the Circus, Opera at "Theatre Tacon," and other amusements attracted large audiences: while services held throughout the day at the Cathedral and other Catholic Churches, were but slimly attended.

As advised, we attended "High Mass" at eight o'clock. On entering the Cathedral we found scarcely fifty worshipers, those mostly women and children, and at no time during the service did the number present exceed one hundred. Highly interesting to us was the pompous entrance of the wealthy, aristocratic families, preceded by their slave, bearing a costly rug, which, being spread on the marble floor, all would kneel upon it, the slave first arranging the ladies' trains.

We observed that rich and poor, black and white, knelt side by side, and well might other denominations emulate the noble example of the Catholic Church in thus exemplifying that "God is no respecter of persons."

Behind the altar rail were about a dozen priests, all of whom took part in the service. In the absence of a choir they chanted the responses with the accompaniment of a fine organ located in the gallery.

Just previous to the ceremony of " Elevating the Host," a priest passed through the congregation motioning all to kneel, and touched upon the shoulder with his staff those who did not immediately comply.

Soon followed a sermon in Spanish, delivered with great rapidity and violent gesticulation, the speaker utterly failing, however, to command the attention of his audience. A brief ceremonial concluded what had impressed us as an exceedingly cold and lifeless service, so unlike Catholic worship in the United States. Later we visited Havana's most fashionable church, " La Merced." The exterior of this edifice is far from imposing, but the interior having recently undergone a thorough transformation, presented a bright and cheerful appearance in contrast with the other churches of the city ; as at the Cathedral, a large majority of those present were ladies, some of them most elegantly dressed, all combining to form an interesting and attractive scene. Having understood that permission of the government had been granted a Baptist clergyman, residing at " Hotel San Carlos," to hold service in its parlor on Sundays, we proceeded there only to find that it had long since been discontinued, and we were confronted with the fact that on the Island of Cuba there was not a single place of Protestant worship.

Back again at our hotel we met some who with us were desirous of acknowledging the mercy and goodness of God, and assembling, as did the disciples of old, in an upper chamber, we realized the fulfillment of that precious promise. " Where two or three are met together in My name, there I will be in the midst of them."

While our recollections of the Sunday are not wholly unpleasant, we cannot forget how flagrantly the day was violated, and though seemingly a contradiction, we assert that there is no Sabbath in Havana. Thankful are we that our laws in this particular are so different ; and may every attempt to destroy the sanctity of the Sabbath in the United States be most earnestly resisted.

Havana and Matanzas are connected by two railroads, a direct route, about sixty miles, the other more circuitous and nearly thirty miles longer.

For the purpose of seeing more of the intervening country, it is quite usual for tourists to go one route, returning by the other, which plan we followed.

On the road by which Union is accessible, there are but two trains daily, 5½ A. M., and 2 P. M.; in order to stop there *en route*, accomplish the visit to a sugar-plantation in the vicinity, and yet reach Matanzas the same day, we were compelled to take the morning train, though why it should start at such an early hour we cannot understand ; fortunately the depot is situated near by "Hotel El Telegrafo," thus lessening the possibility of our being left.

For nearly half an hour after our train started from Havana, the outside world continued shrouded in darkness, but the rising sun gradually revealed to us the beauty and loveliness of the country through which we were passing, a succession of enchanting scenes and most interesting objects being presented as we were whirled along, for although there is much that is provokingly slow on the Island of Cuba, railroad speed cannot be complained of.   Taking advantage of each stoppage, we would step out upon the platform of our car, or perhaps mingle for a moment with the motley crowd gathered at the stations; quite ludicrous to us was the signal for starting the train, a small hand-bell being rung, reminding us of summons to dinner.   We noticed that the locomotive and cars were of American manufacture, the former made at Paterson, N. J.

On all the railroads of Cuba there are the first, second and third-class passenger cars.   From the first, colored persons are excluded; fare four cents a mile; in the third-class, which is patronized almost entirely by negroes and Chinese, one cent a mile is charged, and the cars provided are extremely common, the seats merely rough boards and without backs.   We could discern but little, if any, difference between the first and second-class cars, both being cane-seated, of very ordinary finish, and notwithstanding the presence of ladies, continually filled with dense clouds of tobacco-smoke.

Arriving at Union, we had no difficulty in finding Mr. Morrison, to whom our letter of introduction was addressed.   Upon learning the object of our calling upon him, he suggested that we visit "Las Canes," the estate of Senor John Peoy, about six miles distant, and kindly gave us a letter to the Administrator or Overseer of the plantation; in a few moments the "volante" which had been ordered for us drove up, and we could scarcely refrain from laughing, so odd-looking was the whole turnout. Imagine, dear reader, a gig body slung between, or slightly forward of, two immense wheels, the shafts extending under it and resting upon an axle behind. In the shafts was harnessed a small horse, and at the left side, in long rope traces, another, upon its back, a heavy wooden saddle in which sat the driver, dressed in a flaming red jacket and the balance of what was once a handsome livery—the whole affair presenting a rather worn-out and dilapidated appearance. In Havana we had frequently seen these vehicles, but had never ridden in one. Before proceeding far we discovered the practical use or rather necessity of the "volante" in Cuba, for so horrible the condition of the roads, so wide and deep the ruts, that nothing else could have borne the strain to which our "volante" was subjected.

The road led, as it were, through one vast field of sugar-cane, and on either side, at intervals, could be seen groups of buildings, in size, small villages, the surroundings of some sugar-plantation.

At last "Las Canes" was reached, and upon presenting our letter we received a cordial welcome. The Administrator first took us to an elevated pavilion, from whence he pointed out the boundaries of the estate, comprising thirty-six hundred acres, sixteen hundred and fifty at that time planted in sugar-cane. He informed us that Senor Peoy employed the labor of two hundred slaves and four hundred coolies, of whom sixty were connected with the sugar mill, the remainder attending to the cultivation and

gathering of the cane.  He also stated that the annual production of " Las Canes" is nearly thirty-five
hundred tons of refined sugar, which is packed for
shipment in boxes of four hundred and twenty-five
pounds each.  We then visited the mill and were
shown the ponderous steam engine (made at West
Point, N. Y.,) and all the details of the machinery,
vats, &c., used in the manufacture of sugar, from the
rollers which crush the cane to the centrifugals in
which the sugar is refined.  The very full and clear
explanations of our escort and the engineer, ena-
bling us to clearly comprehend how sugar is made.
Regret was expressed that the works were not in ope-
ration, we being three weeks too early for the grind-
ing season, which commences in that neighborhood
about the middle of December; a great disappoint-
ment to us, we will admit; however, this interesting
sight will be in reservation for us when we again visit
Cuba.  We next walked through the extensive garden
and examined the many rare and curious plants,
trees and flowers which it contained.  We there saw
for the first time a coffee-plant, the grains being enclosed in what resembled, in color and size, a cranberry.  Most wonderful cactus, flowers of the richest
hues, trees loaded with tropical fruits, all claiming
our attention.

Being invited into the mansion, we found a lunch
had been provided; most enjoyable of all were the
luscious oranges which had just been plucked for us.
We were informed that the Grand Duke Alexis had
lunched from the table at which we were seated and
had highly praised the flavor of the fruit offered him.

From the portico we noticed the negroes as they

came from the fields at noon for dinner, also as they
returned in procession to their work, apparently a
cheerful and contented set, their faces wearing a
happy expression, quite in contrast with the morose
and sullen countenances of the coolies. We had
never before been brought in contact with slavery or
the coolie system, hence everything connected with
both was highly interesting to us, and as a special
favor we were permitted to look at their quarters, or
rather to glance into the walled enclosures, inside of
which they are locked at night, slaves and coolies
being kept separate. Afterwards we spent a few moments in the nursery, where were hosts of little negroes, entirely nude, in charge of several old ''aunt-
ies,'' the mothers being allowed to leave the fields
only occasionally during the day to nurse their babes.
Some were in baskets lying fast asleep, not in the
least disturbed by the swarms of flies which literally
covered them ; some just able to walk, while others
were almost large enough to commence work ; the
whole forming a very comical scene, even now, when
brought to mind, compelling us to laugh. Since
1870, by virtue of a Proclamation of Emancipation
(so-called), children born of slave parents are free,
provided the planter is not called upon to support
them, in which case he is entitled to their services
until they reach twenty-one years of age ; by the
same Proclamation, slaves over sixty years old were
declared free. It is very evident that to the enslaved
this proclamation is only a mockery, while it affords
a cloak to the planter in authorizing him to deny his
support to the aged who cannot be of service to him
any longer. The total abolition of slavery on the

Island of Cuba is merely a question of time; already the negroes are manifesting a restless spirit, they require to be governed with the greatest severity, and it is often necessary to shoot the refractory slave. Not many years ago the slaves attached to several estates united in a revolt; now to prevent a recurrence, different days are observed as the Sabbath upon neighboring plantations. The Cuban planters are continually in dread of a general uprising, which, should it occur, would result in the loss of many lives and terrible destruction of property.

The coolies, as most of our readers know, are brought from China, being contracted for there by the planters to serve them eight years, the usual pay being eight dollars per month with food and clothing. They are virtually in a condition of slavery, as when their term of service has expired there is generally a forced renewal of the contract. Coolies are pronounced more profitable to the planters than the slaves, doing more work, hence are in great demand, and their number is increasing each year. As before intimated, they seem very sullen and morose, and the Overseer informed us that they were often inclined to be rebellious; also that at such times, to enforce authority, firearms were unhesitatingly resorted to.

We have stated that the annual production of "Las Canes" is nearly 3500 tons of sugar, which is all refined upon the estate. The sugar crop of the whole island for the last year is estimated at 796,179 tons.

The United States is Cuba's best customer, last year taking 479,373 tons, or 67.05 per cent. of the 714,960 tons exported; also 177,519 hogsheads of molasses, of the 189,333 exported, being 93 76 per cent.

From another very interesting table we learn that our imports from Cuba for the year ending June, 1873, were valued at $77,365,749 mainly sugar, molasses and tobacco as follows: Total sugar and molasses, $66,069,031. Tobacco, $9,678,858. Our exports to the island during the same period amounting to $16,628,788.

We do not propose to discuss the desirability of annexation to the United States, but would remark that it seems almost inevitable that some time in the future, Cuba will come into possession or control of the United States. Visitors to the sugar-plantations of Cuba are sure to receive a welcome, but the attention shown and facilities afforded us at "Las Canes" are quite unusual, particularly as regards the gratification of our curiosity in reference to slaves and coolies. Thanking all for their kindness, not forgetting the Engineer, (a most enthusiastic American, receiving $170 per month, in gold,) we stepped into our "volante," and after another severe jostling, arrived safely at Union, having a little spare time, in which to enjoy the kindly proffered hospitality of Mr. Morrison and his wife, before the departure of the train for Matanzas.

## CHAPTER V.

Matanzas.—"Hotel Leon de Oro."—Our Morning Drive.—Visit to the Caves of the Beautiful Sea.—Valley of the Yumuri.—Returning to Havana.—Our Departure for Home.—The Steamer "City of Wilmington."—A Stormy Voyage.—Some Parting Advice about Visiting Cuba.

THE city of Matanzas, with a population of forty thousand, is next in size and wealth to Havana. The general characteristics of these two cities are the same excepting that the streets of Matanzas are wider and the whole city presents a cleaner and more attractive appearance. Possessing a magnificent harbor and being the terminus of several railroads, which connect it with the principal tobacco and sugar-producing districts of the island, Matanzas has become an important shipping point, and no mean rival of Havana for the commercial supremacy of Cuba. There is comparatively little of interest to the tourist in Matanzas, but its lovely surroundings will fully repay a visit. At the hotel "Leon de Oro" (Lion of Gold,) we experienced the kindest treatment; the gentlemanly proprietor exerting himself to the utmost to render our stay agreeable; his attentions contrasting strongly with the studied indifference usually manifested by landlords in the United States toward their guests. Early in the morning, before breakfast, we started in a volante for "Las Cuevas de Bellamar" ·(the caves of the beautiful sea); for some distance the road led along the shores of the bay, then over some

steep hills, until a broad table land was reached.
There we found a frame shanty built over the entrance of the cave ; silence reigned within, until the
loud ringing of a bell awakened one of the guides,
who arose and admitted us ; ranged around the
building inside were glass cases containing specimens of the crystals, etc., for sale ; and in one corner
of the room a bar, alas, too convenient, it being very
generally patronized by the visitors, particularly after
they have inspected the cave, the exertion and con-
sequent fatigue being made the excuse for partaking
of alcoholic stimulants, nothing milder being kept
there.  Our guide lighted his waxen torch and we
followed him down a very steep stairway into the
cavern ; soon we entered an immense vaulted apartment known as the "Gothic Temple," having massive pillars and arches, also what was pointed out
as the "Organ."  Passing on we saw many more
splendid stalactites and stalagmites, some of most
curious formation, bearing striking resemblance to
owls, cats, monkeys' faces, or vases of flowers, while
to recognize "Columbus' Mantle," "Frozen Water-
fall," "Mother and Babe," and "Cloak of the Vir-
gin," required some slight stretch of the imagination.  After proceeding about one and a half miles,
at which point we were three hundred feet below the
surface, we returned to the entrance by another and
more difficult route, and right glad were we when
the outer world was regained, for, as is the case in
all caves, the heat was almost stifling.  These caves,
though not so extensive as the Mammoth Cave of
Kentucky, are pronounced even more beautiful and
interesting.  There are portions still unexplored, and

even greater wonders may yet be revealed. We can cordially endorse the saying: "He who has not seen the caves of Bellamar has not seen Cuba."

The "valley of the Yumuri" is a narrow gorge, about four miles long. Through it flows a tiny river, from which the valley takes its name; it is seen to greatest advantage from the summit of the "Cumbre," distant from Matanzas four miles. From this point the eye scans the entire valley—clothed in richest verdure, with groups of palms scattered here and there, it is indeed charming and picturesque, such a scene as cannot fail to impress itself upon the mind of the beholder, "a thing of beauty which is a joy forever." Descending the mountain we had a pleasing view of Matanzas, its bay, and, in the distance, old ocean.

Delightful indeed are the recollections of our stay at Matanzas, and fondly do we cherish the desire again to visit that charming locality.

We returned to Havana by the shorter or more direct railroad route, finding it decidedly preferable, there being a greater variety of scenery, while the country showed the highest state of cultivation; all about us the orange-groves, immense sugar estates, vast fields of bananas, and a bewildering array of tropical trees and plants. Arriving at Regla, the town opposite Havana, we took ferry boat, and while crossing the bay had a fine view of the city and its shipping. Seeking again "Hotel el Telegrafo," where we had left our baggage, we remained there in the enjoyment of its comforts, until starting for home. Having obtained the necessary permit to leave the island, we bade adieu to the proprietor and

clerks at the hotel, to whose kindness and considera-
tion we must bear testimony, and proceeded to the
steamer, not, however, before calling at 76 Calle-de-
Cuba, to thank Mr. McKellar for his counsel and aid
to a "stranger in a strange land." Stepping into a
small sail-boat we were soon on board the " *City of
Wilmington*," which lay at anchor about half a mile
from the shore. At last the Cu-tom House officials,
who had been on the steamer since its arrival at Havana, took their departure. All being in readiness,
we steamed slowly out of the harbor, "homeward
bound."

We do not purpose entering into the details of our
return voyage, but cannot forbear an acknowledgment of the kind attentions shown us by Captain
Reed and all others connected with the "*City of
Wilmington.*"

We were denied the delightful weather which made
our outward passage so pleasant. Scarcely had the
coast of Cuba faded from view when a storm arose,
and, continuing until our destination was reached,
interfered greatly with our comfort and enjoyment;
but the opportunity afforded us of witnessing, in all its
terrible grandeur, a storm at sea, was ample compen-
sation. As we proceeded northward the temperature
gradually lowered, until tropical heat was exchanged
for the chilliness of winter. Repeating the introduction to our first article :

Thursday, November 27th, we bid adieu to Cuba,
its tropical greenness and beauty; five days later
we see the snow-clad highlands of New York and
are chilled by winter's icy breath. In visiting the
"Queen of the Antilles," the land of orange-grove

and palm, a long-cherished desire has been gratified, and our fullest expectations met in its strange
sights and luxuriant growth, our enjoyment marred
only by the sad, sad picture of "Man's inhumanity
to man," the cruelty, ignorance and degradation so
prevalent throughout the Island of Cuba. Returning
to the United States, more than ever do we appreciate the blessing of civil and religious liberty, and
deeply grateful are we that our lot has been cast in
a Christian land.

Our parting advice, dear reader, is, *visit Cuba;*
nowhere on the face of the globe do customs and
manners contrast more strongly with our own, nowhere is everything more quaint and strange. As a
*foreign* trip, all things considered, particularly time
and expense, "TO CUBA AND BACK IN TWENTY-TWO
DAYS" is unsurpassed. The ocean voyage will
strengthen and invigorate, and you will be charmed
with the beauty and loveliness of the tropical isle.
Yes, go to Cuba, and you will discover that our
description is not exaggerated—rather "that the half
has not been told."

**THE END.**

## NOTE.

We must not be understood as advising a visit to Cuba during the summer months, or until every trace of the yellow fever has disappeared, usually not before November. A very suitable time to visit the island is about the middle of December, when the heat has moderated and sugar-making upon the plantations is at its height; or, delaying the visit until February, be in Havana during the " Carnival," which is described as very amusing. The present disturbed state of affairs in Cuba is likely to continue, possibly to increase, but one need not venture too near the theatre of operations, and by abstaining from the expression of any opinion upon the merits of the rebellion, can avoid everything like insult or danger.

www.ingramcontent.com/pod-product-compliance
Lightning Source LLC
Chambersburg PA
CBHW021437090426
42739CB00009B/1527